T0196595

A STRATEGIC CREATOR
Scientific Concepts and the Bible

Divinely Designed 2

RACHEL FORD STEPHENS

authorHOUSE®

AuthorHouse™
1663 Liberty Drive
Bloomington, IN 47403
www.authorhouse.com
Phone: 1 (800) 839-8640

Published by AuthorHouse 12/11/2018

ISBN: 978-1-5462-6991-5 (sc)
ISBN: 978-1-5462-6990-8 (e)

Print information available on the last page.

This book is printed on acid-free paper.

A STRATEGIC CREATOR

Scientific Concepts and the Bible

divinely designed

DEDICATION

This book is dedicated to my humorous and brilliantly creative grandchildren who loving refer to me as "Big Mama":

Berkeley Imani Stephens

Aubrey Malia Stephens

Iris Rachel Stephens

Titus William Stephens

DIVINELY DESIGNED 2

A STRATEGIC CREATOR
Scientific Concepts and the Bible
(Work/Coloring Book)

Suggestions for Usages

This book consists of pages to color, aligned with a study of science relative to biblical scripture. Although coloring is optional, a scientific mind would be intrigued to explore and promote further studies.

The pages to color are doodles done during the writing of the book. Doodling space is provided for you in the margins to help internalize studied concepts.

It can also be used as a personal journal study or a group study, in a science classroom/lab, in your church bible study, and as the subject of a conference.

DIVINELY DESIGNED 2

A STRATEGIC CREATOR
Scientific Concepts and the Bible
(Work/Coloring Book)

CONTENTS

DIVINELY DESIGNED 2

A STRATEGIC CREATOR
Scientific Concepts and the Bible

Introduction: Truth and Reality

"For as he thinketh in his heart, so is he:... ."
Proverbs 23:7

'In this book we will look at some scientific concepts and compare them with biblical scripture. My goal is to establish truth as it relates to Christianity through the strategic nature of God and give the Christian additional evidence to defend their faith. Just to make a point of how a person's truth can be distorted, I will begin with a familiar fictional movie, *The Wizard of Oz*.

In the movie *The Wizard of Oz*, Dorothy throws water on the Wicked Witch of the West. The water melted the Wicked Witch. As she was melting she cried, "What a world. What a world. Who would've thought a good little girl like you could destroy my beautiful wickedness?" The Wicked Witch saw her wickedness as being beautiful. It was how she saw her world. It was her reality. It was her truth.

How do you see this world? However you see it that defines your world view. Everyone has a world view, whether it is good or bad; a world view is the sum total of all that a person believes about the world. It has been shaped and is being shaped by our experiences, teachings, and what we see and hear. Social media and television play a large part in shaping your world view. They determine how you make decisions and establish your lifestyle. The worldly claims of truth give the impression that one can live anyway and still have a good end. It gives no bases for distinguishing good from bad, steadfastness, or hope. The Wicked Witch of the West had a world view. I proposed to you that your ending – where you spend eternity-will be determined by your world view, good or bad. As you develop your world view try examining the world through the eyes of a strategic creator.

Growing up, my family always attended church. My parents generously served in many capacities. My Daddy sang with a quartet, was the church musician and superintendent of the Sunday School. My Mother was the church secretary and head of the usher board ministry. We learned the Catechism, a manual on biblical doctrine, and attended Sunday School and bible study unwaveringly. During every Spring and Fall Revival, we were required to sit on the mourners' bench. The mourners' bench is where you sat if you wanted to receive salvation. After the preacher had preached a soul-stirring sermon, we prayed and cried out for salvation. When I entered college I fully employed these teachings. They were the lens through which I envisioned my truth.

During my freshman year, I went through what I considered a major crisis. Although I do not wish to share the details of the crisis, believe, it was a great struggle. I encountered people that had different world views. My parents were not there to console and protect me. What was I to do? One day, I reached a point where the struggle was more than I could bear. Late one night, I went to the college's chapel, which was open 24 hours every day. On that mourner's bench I had learned how to cry out to God. For me, during my youth, the cry was salvation. I needed salvation from my sins. But that night, I needed salvation from this crisis. While on my knees, at the altar, I cried out to God. I said, "If you don't take this thing from me, I will not make it. I'm not leaving this place until you do." I stayed there and talked with God for two hours.

I had always been under the protective umbrella of my loving and caring parents. My truth had never been put on trial. At that point, I needed to know that all the teachings I received were true and were going to pull me through this crisis. I needed to know He was faithful to His word and that all His promises were truly yea and amen. That night, I learned without question that TRUTH is able to do what it says it can do. When I rose from my knees, I was totally freed from the pain. Even today, I can barely remember the anguish I suffered.

Through the study of science, I can see the strategic design of God and how it reveals a truthful reality. It is not just information; it is an entire life walk with God. It can be lived daily. I have also learned TRUTH is dependable and consistent and more than anything it reveals who God IS.

I often think about what would have happened to me if I had a world view not based on the teachings of the bible. What would have happened if I did not know the truth. Would I have had a breakdown and be mentally unstable today? Or would I have turned to other means to soothe the pain.

All sixteen chapters of this book reveal different strategies of God as it pertains to man. These sixteen chapters are not even close to the entire plan of God. As you read these strategic plans of the creator, revealing the truthfulness of the bible, it is my prayers that these brief lessons on the scientific concepts that are compared with biblical scripture will do for you what that night on my knees on the altar did for me and that is, confirm the TRUTH!

1. IN THE BEGINNING

"In the beginning God created the heaven and the earth."
Genesis 1: 1

Genesis 1:1 gives the first words of the Bible, "In the beginning…." It clearly tells us that there was a beginning. The Law of Causality states if anything had a beginning it also had a cause. Science is in agreement with the first three words of the Bible, there was a beginning. Just what the cause of the beginning was and is the source of disagreement.

The Big Bang Theory is the most popular theory of how the universe had its beginning. This scientific belief was created when it was observed that the galaxies are moving away from the Milky Way at a great speed in all directions. The Milky Way is the galaxy where our solar system exists. It is believed that before the Big Bang all matter and energy were compressed into a hot, dense mass just a few millimeters across and it all happened in a trillion-trillionth of a second.[1]

Whenever there is a great amount of energy released in a chemical reaction it is usually accompanied with a great sound, hence the Big Bang. Could the sound have been the voice of God? In the book of Exodus, God's voice is described as being a trumpet that sounded louder and louder (Exodus 19: 16, 19). The author of the book of Job went further in describing the voice of God. He states, "God thundereth marvelously with his voice: great things doeth he, which we cannot comprehend."

The Bible had spoken of the spreading of the universe before it was suggested by the Big Bang Theorist. "God coverest Himself with light as with a garment and stretched out the heavens like a curtain." (Psalm 104: 2) "He stretched out the heavens as a curtain and spreadeth them out as a tent to dwell in." (Isaiah 40: 2) The suffix –*eth*, at the end of words, tells us that it is a continuing process. God is still spreading and stretching. The very thing, the galaxies moving away from the Milky Way, that caused science to come up the Big Bang Theory, is no more than God spreading the heavens. "The tent to dwell in", tells us that conditions were made and are being made for our dwelling. The spreading and stretching is necessary for our galaxy, The Milky Way, among other galaxies, to be suitable for our planet Earth to exist. Even our location on the outer arm of our galaxy is necessary.

Evolutionist suggests the universe will continue to spread until it uses up all its energy. Then it will contract into its original mass and explode, repeating the process over again. This theory, The Oscillating Theory, suggests a new Heaven and a new Earth. John wrote in the book of Revelation, "And I saw a new heaven and a new earth: for the first heaven and the first earth were passed away: and there was no more sea. And I, John saw the holy city, New Jerusalem, coming down from God out of heaven saying, Behold, the tabernacle of God is with men, and he will dwell with them, and they shall be his people, and God himself shall be with them, and be their God."

Your faith, your worldview should give you an answer to your beginning. Take the time and consider your worldview as it pertains to your origin.

My Thoughts:
Your worldview should answer three very important questions: Where did I come from? Why am I here? Where am I going?

If someone is having a problem with how the Earth had its beginning, they may also be having a problem with their own beginning. If someone is having a problem with why they are here, they may be having a problem with their purpose. And if someone is having a problem with where they are going then they may be having a problem with their destiny.

Some believe in evolution, the process by which a species change to the point it loses its existence. Consider the following questions as you ponder on your world view. If evolution is your belief then how does it answer the important questions? If your existence is only to create a higher life form, then what determines your value and your worth? Then why have emotions that cause you to wonder and search for the more in life?

Your Thoughts:

_____

_____

_____

_____

_____

_____

_____

_____

2. AND THERE WAS LIGHT

"And God said, Let there be light: and there was light."
Genesis 1: 3

The first thing on God's agenda after He created heaven and earth was the creation of light and He called it good. In chapter 13, I will discuss why He called His creation good. For now let's look at why He made light His first creation after heaven and earth. Light is energy. Energy is a measurable property that is transferred to an object in order to do work, cause change, or heat an object. It had to be first in order to obtain the energy that would propel and sustain creation. Energy is necessary to hold the protons and neutrons together in the nuclei of atoms in which all matter consist. And as the atoms combine to form compounds, energy is trapped in their chemical bonds.

God did not need light to see or observe His creation, but rather to form atoms and compounds that are the basis for everything created. Hebrews 11: 3 states, "… so that things (living and nonliving) which are seen were not made of things which do appear." With an endless supply of energy/light things (living and nonliving) could appear from things which are not seen. Energy and atoms cannot be seen with the naked eye. And energy is never destroyed but can be changed from one form to another.

Light is also necessary for the process of photosynthesis. This process supplies all living things with food, whether directly or indirectly.

First John 1: 5, "This then is the message which we have heard of Him, and declare unto you, that God is light and in Him is not darkness at all." Meditate on Jesus being the "light" of the world.

My Thoughts:

The Word of God brings life (light) to any situation. This is because the Word is living and darkness implies death or dying. Add the Word of God to a hopeless situation and hope is restored. The word of God brings life to any dire situation.

In Revelation 22:5, John wrote, "And there shall be no night there; and they need no candle, neither light of the sun; for the Lord God giveth them light: and they shall reign forever and ever." This scripture tells us that not only is God the spiritual light of all situations and occasions of our lives but He is also the light of our physical light. TThere will come a day when there will be no need for any light outside of Him.

This goes further to suggest that there will be no light in Hell. However, there may be fire and brimstone but there will be no light. The only light will be where He is present. **Without Him, NO light will be possible.**

Your Thoughts:

_____

_____

_____

_____

3. ALL THE WATER IN ONE PLACE

"And God said, Let the waters under the heaven be gathered together unto one place, and let the dry land appear: and it was so. And God called the dry land Earth; and the gathering together of the waters called he Seas: and God saw that it was good."
Genesis 1: 9, 10

In the scripture reference, we see God called all the water into one place. If all the water was in one place, then all the land was in one place, creating one continent….. one supercontinent, Pangaea (Pangea).

The story of Noah and the flood is told in Genesis, chapters 6 – 10. In chapter 10, after the flood, the generations of the sons of Noah, Shem, Ham, and Japheth, are listed. In verse 25, it states, "… for in his days was the earth divided." Commentators have written that this refers to the dividing of the generations of Noah; however, in verse 32 after the complete listings of the generations it states, "These are the families of the sons of Noah, after their generations, in their nations: and by these were the nations divided in the earth after the flood."

The dividing of the earth in verse 25 is the separating of Earth's plates. This is plate tectonics. In the theory of Plate Tectonics, the Earth's crust is believe to be composed of many individual plates that have changed shape and position over time. These plates made it possible for the Earth to divide as stated in Genesis 10: 25. The separation of Pangaea into continents shows divine design and strategy.

Think on why God separated the land into continents. What would life be like if the land had remained one continent? Would there still be racism? How different or alike would we be?

My Thoughts:

Separating the land was a strategic move by a very wise and all-knowing God. By separating the land, water could surround the land creating a natural coolant for the land.

When God created water, He created it with a high specific heat – absorbing heat/energy without a great raise in temperature. If you have ever visited the beach on a hot summer day I'm sure you noticed the temperature difference between the hot sand (low specific heat) and the cold water (high specific heat). As the Earth turns on tilted axis and creating four seasons, a summer season could have a devastating effect, especially along the Equator where it is hot year round. Regardless of the heat, God's creation of water absorbs the heat maintaining a livable Earth.

His strategic plan for water did not stop there. He created our bodies with 70% water, just like our Earth's surface which is 70% water, to absorb heat produced by the metabolic processes within us. One can feel the effects of increase metabolic processes when there is fever produced from a sickness.

In addition to God strategically placing the continents, allow me to say one land mass would not have prevented the different races. There were prejudices between Jews, Gentiles, Samaritans, and others. North America, South America, Australia, large parts of Eurasia, and Africa had not yet been inhabited.

Racism has nothing to do with separation. "Out of the mouth flows the issues of the heart." It is a heart condition.

Your Thoughts:

_____
_____
_____
_____
_____
_____
_____

4. HE PREPARED THE SOIL

"And the Lord God formed man of the dust of the ground, and breathed into his nostrils the breath of life; and man became a living soul."
Genesis 2: 7

Paul wrote in Corinthians, "Let all things be done properly and with order." God is not a God of disorder or confusion. He does things in order. In Genesis, the order of God's creation had purpose. In this topic, we will consider the order in which plants were established on earth. In ecology, the study of the environment, this order is called succession.

Succession is the gradual replacement of one type of ecological community by another in the same area, involving a series of orderly changes. As one ecological community grows, it prepares the soil for a more prominent community by adding additional nutrients to the soil. In Genesis 1: 11, we see God establishing the order for plant succession, "And God said, Let the earth bring forth grass, the herb yielding seed, and the fruit tree yielding fruit after his kind, whose seed is in itself, upon the earth: and it was so." Grass, shrubs, and trees is the order of succession. While God was preparing the environment for man's survival, He was also preparing the soil for man's creation.

17

When the soil had been thoroughly prepared through succession, God formed man from the dust of the ground. The earth had been prepared.

Some teach that our different races come from the different colors of soil. We do not read God returning to the soil to create man again. There is only one race of people, the human race. What does your world view say in response to this statement?

My Thoughts:

I would have loved to have observed my God actually molding and shaping man. He referred to Himself as the Potter and we are the clay in His hands, generating a virtual image of the Potter on the Potter's wheel. With God as the potter, it was more than Him putting soil (clay – small, fine grains of dirt) on top of soil. As He was shaping He was creating cells with organelles to carry out the various metabolic reactions for a functioning body. He was creating deoxyribonucleic acid (DNA) and ribonucleic acid (RNA) to store this information so that it could be repeated throughout man existence. How did He form the hair, nails, eyes, ears, teeth, tongue, etc.? How did He separate bones, blood, and flesh and give each of us our very own distinctive fingerprints? And how particular He must have been when it came to creating the "blood". He did it with purpose in mind …. His death, burial, and resurrection.

Ephesians 2: 10 declare, "For we are His workmanship, created in Christ Jesus unto good works, which God hath before ordained that we should walk in them." **What a grand event that must have been!!!**

Your thoughts:

_____
_____
_____
_____
_____
_____
_____

5. EARTH'S POSITION

"And God said, Let there be lights in the firmament of heaven to divide the day from the night; and let them be for signs, and for seasons, and for days, and years. And let them be for lights in the firmament of the heaven to give light upon the earth: and it was so. And God made two great lights; the greater light to rule the day, and the lesser light to rule the night: he made the stars also. And God set them in the firmament of the heaven to give light upon the earth. And to rule over the day and over the night, and to divide the light from darkness: and God saw that it was good."

Genesis 1: 14 – 18

As mentioned in chapter one, the tent to dwell in stated in Isaiah 40:2, tells us that conditions were made and are being made for our dwelling. The spreading and stretching is necessary for our galaxy, The Milky Way, among other galaxies, to be suitable for our planet Earth to exist.

Sir Isaac Newton's Law of Universal Gravitation states that every object in the universe attracts every other object. Gravitational force is an attractive force that acts between any two masses and is proportional to their masses and decreases rapidly as the distance between the masses increases: the greater the masses, the greater the gravitational force between the objects and the closer the masses the greater the gravitational force.

This gravitational force keeps our planet in orbit around our sun. It is also responsible for keeping our moon in orbit around our planet and results in the low and high tides in our oceans.

The rate of expansion or spreading of the universe happens only at the appropriate speed. If the expansion is too fast, the gravitational forces would be too weak and stars would not form and there would be no planets. If the expansion is too slow, gravitational forces would be too great and bits and pieces of cosmic matter would coagulate, resulting in black holes and no planets.

Earth's location on the outer arm of the Milky Way, a spiral galaxy, is important. First, if our galaxy was an irregular galaxy, it would be too small. There would be too much pull from the other galaxies, making it unstable. Secondly, too large of a disc in the galaxy would form black holes. And thirdly, our galaxy must be of medium size and our location had to be on the outer arm for us to be safe from the gravitational pull of the other galaxies.[2]

Physicists have tried to mimic gravity and its forces on the structure of our universe. Man, with all his knowledge, resources, and inventiveness have not come close to what the Designer has done. The precision in the spacing and placing of matter for our existence has lead physicists to conclude there must be a Divine Designer or should I say a Strategic Creator. The Lord said in Jeremiah 33: 35, "I have appointed the ordinances of heaven and earth." He has fixed laws, a strategy governing heaven and earth.

Consider the location of our planet in the solar system. Discuss other ways God has created a tent for us to dwell in or made us safe.

My Thoughts:

In my excitement about this book, I shared a few things about the strategic plan of our Creator, with a certain individual. I shared my thoughts on how He strategically placed us so that we could view His creation free from the debris of the universe. IIn the midst of the conversation, the individual said man has to have a very big ego to think that

Earth is the only planet in the universe to have life and that God would do all this just for Earth.

Well, I was not expecting that. I responded, "You must not think much of God to think that He is not able." Job 11:7, 8, 9 says "Canst thou by searching find out God? Canst thou find out the Almighty unto perfection? It is as high as heaven: what canst thou do? Deeper than hell; what canst thou know? The measure thereof is longer than the earth, and broader than the sea." **God has no limits!**

Yes my ego, when it comes to my God, is greater than huge. Especially when I think of how He went to the cross just for me.

Your Thoughts:

_____

_____

_____

_____

_____

_____

_____

6. THE SEED

"And God said, Let the earth bring forth grass, the herb yielding seed, and the fruit tree yielding fruit after his kind, whose seed is in itself, upon the earth: and it was so. And the earth brought forth grass, and herb yielding seed after his kind, and the tree yielding fruit, whose seed was in itself, after his kind: and God saw it was good."

Genesis 1: 11, 12

A seed has in it everything it needs to become the intended plant. Inside the seed is an embryonic plant with all it parts and a source of energy to begin growth. As it is in the natural, so it is in the spirit. Whenever a seed is mentioned in scripture and it is not referenced to a seed of a plant; it signifies that the seed has everything necessary to establish its purpose.

In John 1: 1, God is the Word and in Luke 8: 11, the seed is the Word. If a seed has within it all it is to become, then the Word has all within it to become what it is spoken to be. That is why the Word will not return unto Him void. It will establish its purpose. It can only become what is in it.

When the Word is spoken into your life, it has to be fulfilled. Watch your words; you could be planting negative seeds that will produce bad fruit.

 Talk over words that have been spoken into your life and any manifestation of them whether positive or negative.

29

My Thoughts:

I have been careful with the influence that has been given to me, as a mother and as an educator for over forty years. I realized the power of words. Many times when I encounter former students, they tell me how my words have made a difference in their life.

My biological children were told from birth, "You are destined for greatness." I witness it unfolding before me each day. To God be the glory.

I have not always been where I am now. Thank God for the many mentors that have spoken words of encouragement. Of the many words, there was one statement spoken by my pastor, Bishop Michael A. Blue, which provoked me more than others. He said one Sunday morning, "You are not the you, you are going to be." Just knowing circumstances and situations will not be this way always; did wonders for me as a person.

I do not view aging as becoming nonproductive. I see it now as using my gifts in a different and more creative way. Maya Angelou said that with each decade, her life became more and more fulfilling.

I am excited and anxious to see what God is going to do in the next chapter of my life.

Your Thoughts:

_____
_____
_____
_____
_____
_____
_____

7. THE SEED OF THE WOMAN

"And I will put enmity between thee and the woman, and between thy seed and her seed; it shall bruise thy head, and thou shall bruise his heel."
Genesis 3:15

In the referenced verse, God is speaking to the serpent in the Garden of Eden after he had tempted Adam and Eve to eat of the fruit from the forbidden tree of life. The serpent apparently thought he was victorious in destroying God's plan for man. Here, God is informing Satan that even though he used the woman, it will be her seed that will bring his end.

In the previous lesson, we learned that a seed has in it all that it needs to become what it is to be. Well, the woman's seed also has the same properties, although in this case, the woman's seed is Jesus. When God created the woman, He created her with a womb able to house Jesus. It had to be a womb that could birth a Savior with pure blood to redeem humanity and reestablish humanity's relationship with the Father.

How did He do it? First, the womb was built so that the blood of the mother and baby would not mix. So He created a womb where the blood vessels of the uterine lining would interlock with the blood vessels of the placenta to which the baby was connected. The closeness of the blood vessels allows nutrients and oxygen, through the process of diffusion, to diffuse from the mother's blood

into the baby's blood. And water through osmosis could pass from the mother's blood and the baby's blood. The placenta is derived from the fertilized egg and not from the mother's womb.

Secondly, all cells in the human body have a nucleus, with the exception of mature red blood cells. No nucleus in the cell means no DNA, no DNA means none of the mother will be in the cell. This means none of Mary would be in Jesus' red blood. Therefore, when His blood was shed, His blood would be pure, and only pure blood would be able to wash away the sins of an entire humanity.

Human blood cells live about one hundred twenty days but the blood of Jesus continues to last for over two thousand years.

 Discuss the saving power of the blood of Jesus.

My Thoughts:

Jesus said in John 3:16, "For God so loved the world that He gave His only begotten Son, that whosoever believeth in him should not perish, but have everlasting life." I continually see how God loves me so and how He so loved this world. His plan for my salvation was not a last minute afterthought. He had every detail on His mind when He said "Let us make man in our image...."

Our sins are so great He made sure His blood would be pure and NO one would be lost. He presented an Isaiah 57:5 situation that would cover all points of view concerning salvation. It says, "But He was wounded for our transgressions, He was bruised for our iniquities: the chastisement of our peace was upon Him; and with His stripes we are healed."

He made it so that all we have to do is confess with our mouth the Lord Jesus, and believe in our hearts that God raised Him from the dead and we are saved.

Your Thoughts:

_____
_____
_____
_____
_____
_____
_____

8. CREATED TO PRAISE

*"Let everything that hath breath praise
the LORD. Praise ye the LORD."*
Psalm 150: 6

God never gave a command without giving the means to fulfill it. When he gave the Ten Commandments, He had already given the people what they would need to keep them. In the first four commandments, He said to have no other gods before Him, and no graven images, not to bow to them, and not to take His name in vain. To be able to keep these four, He gave Himself, the God who is able to do exceeding abundantly all you could think or ask. All things are possible in Him. The fifth commandment says to remember the Sabbath day and keep it holy. He gave a week which included a weekend for all work so that the Sabbath is free for rest and worship. In the sixth commandment, He says to honor your mother and father, so he gave parents who would create us out of love and love us unconditionally before we could know ourselves. The seventh commandment says not to kill; He gave the ability to love. In love, there is forgiveness and the ability to let go of anger. He gave a husband and wife so there would not be adultery. He said ask and we shall have and there would be no need to steal. He gave us truth so we do not have to lie. And why would you even want your neighbor's possessions when He said He came so that we might have life and have it abundantly?

He also said to praise Him, so like the commandments He also gave us what we needed to praise. He went further than giving us hands to clap and the ability to play instruments, feet to dance, and mouths to shout, He also put praise within us. Praise moves God. Psalm 22:3 tells us that God inhabits the praise of His people. Our praise is sweet savor to His nostrils. He enjoys the praises of His people, so God put in us a praise that is ongoing, constant, and always. He put our praise in our DNA.

In a biology seminar at the University of North Carolina at Pembroke, the presenter was offering the latest information on the DNA molecule. He stated that when musical notes were assigned to the nitrogenous bases (thymine, adenine, guanine, and cytosine), they produced music. Now, I understand why the psalmist wrote in the last verse of the Psalms, Let everything that hath breath praise the LORD. Praise ye the LORD." The praise is within, the core of our existence. This was not an accident of evolution.

Music is a part of our very being. We cannot help but move when we hear music. It is virtually impossible to be motionless when listening to music.

Music begins celebrations, morning worship, and athletic events. Music also begins documentaries, cartoons and movies have musical themes. Advertisements have jingles and weddings are full of emotions in songs. We teach our children in songs. We learned our ABC's and nursery rhymes with music. Music moves us, dramatically.

Our praise was determined by God at our conception. He knows our life stories and what songs we would need. Each of us began life as a single fertilized egg, a zygote, with one set of DNA, coding many songs. That zygote reproduced into trillions of cells, all having the same DNA, the same praise.

He has given us the ability to praise Him with every fiber of our being! Psalm 139: 14 states, "I will praise thee; for I am fearfully and wonderfully made: marvelous are thy works; and that my soul knoweth right well."

Discuss songs that you enjoy and ones enjoyed by others. Also discuss a song(s) that means a lot to you but not to others. Could this be because of the DNA that makes you different?

My Thoughts:

For the most part, everyone's DNA is the same. We each walk on two legs, we have two arms, our eyes are in the front of our faces, we have ten fingers and ten toes, and therefore, much of our DNA is similar. Those songs are the same. Perhaps, these songs are our daily blessings of life, health, and strength.

But there is DNA that makes you different from anyone else in the world. This DNA codes those special songs that move you. Our struggles are different, the problems that we face daily and go through are not the same, so our songs need to be different. Those songs make your sorrow turn to tears of joy. When you hear a special song that quicken in you, that song relates to your DNA.

That song was your praise for your situation. When you hear a certain song you may not remember but one line; that's all you need. DNA is handling the rest.

Some cells, like your muscles, have multiple sets of DNA. They work the hardest, so they need extra praise. The harder the struggle you come through, the greater the praise.

Your Thoughts:

_____

_____

_____

_____

_____

_____

_____

9. NO JUNK DNA

"For my thoughts are not your thoughts, neither are your ways my ways, saith the LORD. For as the heavens are higher that the earth, so are my ways higher than your ways, and my thoughts than your thoughts."
Isaiah 55: 8, 9

The DNA code has to be carried from the nucleus of the cell to organelles in the cytoplasm (outside the nucleus) called ribosomes. On the ribosomes, proteins are built to make us who we are through a process called protein synthesis, which is carried out by DNA and RNA. Protein synthesis involves the DNA code being given to messenger RNA (mRNA) through a process called transcription. During transcription mRNA receives all the code of DNA; however, not all the code is to be carried to the ribosomes. Only the part that consists of exons is to be carried to the ribosomes, for this is the part that is to be expressed in protein synthesis. The part not carried consists of introns; this unexpressed part is cut away during RNA splicing. The introns were thought to be left over from evolution and were cut out so they would not be expressed.

These introns are now believed to be critical in that they code small or micro RNA. The three-dimensional shape of the nucleus is maintained by a skeleton created by small or micro RNA. Introns also play a role in the actual splicing of mRNA[3].

Scientists also believe introns buffer DNA from mutations. Mutations are changes in the DNA code. Mutations have become a part of DNA since the fall of man in the Garden of Eden. Genetic diseases and disorders are the result of mutations that tend to shorten the life span. Second Corinthians 4: 12 states death works in us. In Chapter 5 of Genesis, man lived over nine centuries. By Genesis 6: 3, God had shortened the life span of man to one hundred twenty years because of sin.

Could it be that what science does not understands or misunderstands, in time may point to the divine design of our creator?

Talk about specific mutations that have shortened the life span of man. Could death be God's way of limiting sin on the planet?

My Thoughts:

In the third chapter of Ecclesiastes Solomon wrote, "To every thing there is a season, and a time to every purpose under the heaven. A time to be born, and a time to die; ..."

I do not believe that mutations that result in disease are of God. However, our omniscient God has providence all events would be worked out according to His purpose. His knowledge is beyond our truths.

Your Thoughts:

_____
_____
_____
_____
_____
_____

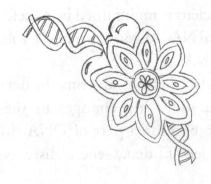

10. LEFT HANDED AMINO ACIDS

"These are the generations of the heavens and of the earth when they were created, in the day that the LORD God made the earth and the heavens."
Genesis 2: 4

Scientists believe that the Earth was very hot when it was first formed. There were great earthquakes and volcano eruptions as the Earth took its shape. Also, the Earth spent about two billion years cooling down by thunderstorms and heavy rains, hence the formation of the seas.

Alexander I. Oparin, in the 1930's, proposed a theory of how life began. He believed during this cooling down period life began in the seas. He explained how the primitive atmosphere consisted of water vapor (H_2O) formed when the rains hit the hot surface of the Earth. Methane (CH_4), Nitrogen (N_2), and hydrogen (H_2) were thrown into the atmosphere by volcanoes. Lightning from the thunderstorms split these molecules and supplied energy for the proceeding chemical reactions. These reactions formed the first amino acids that joined to form proteins and eventually the first cells.

In 1953, Stanley Miller and Harold Urey simulated the conditions of a primitive atmosphere, as proposed by Oparin, in the laboratory and found that life could have begun that way; amino acids were formed[4]. This all sounds believable until further analysis by modern science. The proteins produced in the laboratory were not usable

51

proteins. Amino acids will bond in anyway yielding them nonfunctioning.

Amino acids come in two types, left-handed and right-handed. Almost all life on earth is based on left-handed amino acids. The amino acids produced in the Urey-Miller experiment were right-handed; therefore they could not have begun the process of life.

Science has now found that there are certain bacteria that can convert sugars and right-handed amino acids into left-handed amino acids. This may sound promising to a naturalist but you must remember that bacteria are cells too and would need to be formed before the amino acids to be rendered beneficial.

Schools have not changed science books even though sufficient data exist to prove that some theories are untrue. What are some things that could be done to support the teaching of truth in our schools?

My Thoughts:

Schools may never come to the point where the "truth" is printed in the text books. So it becomes the job of the home and the church to educate our children. Teach them the truth and allow them to learn the scientific concepts taught in school. Knowing the other points of view will allow them to become better witnesses to the truth.

Your Thoughts:

_____
_____
_____
_____
_____
_____
_____

a typical Cell

11. THE CELL

"So God created man in his own image, in the image of God created he him; male and female created he them."
Genesis 1: 27

In this lesson, we will briefly discuss the formation of the cell. In the previous lesson we discussed amino acids, the building blocks of life. Amino acids bind together to form proteins. The number of amino acids it takes to produce one protein is a gene. Most cells' genetic information is on chromosomes. As humans, we have 23 pairs of chromosomes. Each chromosome contains hundreds to thousands of genes.

A group of biologists and computer scientists in Japan created a computer model of a cell. They called it the "bare bones" model. They discovered that a basic cell needed at least 127 genes to be considered a cell, for this to randomly happen scientist have deemed it impossible.

The cell consists of smaller parts called organelles, small organs. Which organelle would have formed first? Could it have been the complex deoxyribonucleic acid (DNA) or the more unstable ribonucleic acid (RNA)? Could the protein have formed first and the DNA and RNA formed from it? Or even yet, could the cell itself with its protein membrane formed first?

Science has concluded that the only possible solution is that they all must have formed at the same time. How could this be, except for the existence of a creator?

💡 Do you find it easier to have faith in God as your creator or to have faith in the cell as a random accident?

My Thoughts:

I enjoy reading and listening to people's stories of how their lives were transformed when they accepted Christ as their Lord and Savior. Drug addicts in and out of rehabilitation centers, alcoholics not able to resist the weekend call to drink, and those striving to resist other addictions often tell how they were unable to be rehabilitated until they found Christ. There is power in the redemptive blood of Jesus.

I find reassurance when hearing or reading their stories of how they not only stop their habits but they found purpose in their lives.

Without Christ their habit is put on pause, with Christ they hit the delete button and they are able to carry on a productive life.

Your Thoughts:

_____

_____

_____

_____

_____

12. HE CALLED IT ALL GOOD

Genesis 1

At the end of each day of creation, God called it good. To be good means that whatever you are referring to has in it all it needs to be whatever it is called to be.

God made creation so that it would maintain and sustain itself until the coming of a new Earth and a new Heaven, therefore it is good.

The law of conservation of mass/matter states that matter is neither created nor destroyed. All matter on Earth was created when God said, "Let there be … and no new matter has been created since. The sun supplies a constant supply of energy but no matter is added to our Earth. Energy is not considered matter for it takes up no space and has not weight. The water used for drinking and bathing and the soil for planting are the same water and soil that were created in chapter 1 of Genesis. Oxygen, nitrogen, carbon are all recycled along with water and soil.

 God considered His work good because He had put into it resilience and sustainability. Are there things in your life you consider good? Why?

My Thoughts:
In the parable of The Talents (Matthew 25: 14 – 30), a man gave to his servants one, two, and five talents. He gave to them according to their ability. While he was away the

one with five talents doubled his to ten. The servant that was given two talents doubled his to four. Their lord said to each of them, "Well done thou good and faithful servant; thou has been faithful over a few things I will make you ruler over many things: enter thou into joy of thy lord."

But the one that was given one talent made no increase. His lord called him wicked, slothful and unprofitable.

The two faithful servants were called good because they took what their lord had given them and showed a substantial increase. It had nothing to do with the amount each had, it had everything to do with their ability and their willingness to use it to the glory of their lord. They each received the same reward. The one that did nothing did not receive a good reward.

It's only good when it does what it is sent to accomplish.

Your Thoughts:

_____

_____

_____

_____

_____

_____

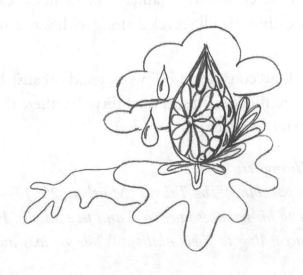

13. HE DID IT IN SEVEN DAYS

Genesis 1

Which came first, the chicken or the egg? How unaware can one be? Of course the chicken came first. God created each living thing with its seed or its ability to reproduce within it. The egg is the result of the reproduction process, and not the beginning of it.

God created the plants in their adult stage. Trees that would have taken years to mature or forests to reach their climax, God created in one day. In verses 11 and 12 of Genesis 1 it states, "… the herb yielding seed and the fruit tree yielding fruit."

He created man in his adult stage, He did not have to go through forty weeks of gestation or the sixteen years or so required in becoming a man. Man in his beginning looked like he had been here for years. He had every cell, every organ, and every organ system.

Just as God created the living things in one day as though they had gone through months, years, and decades, He also created the Earth the same way. The layers in Earth's crust were made when God created the Earth. Science has dated Earth as being 4.6 billion years old. Now scientists are finding fault in their dating and learning that the Earth may not be as old as they once thought.

Why do we see changes that Charles Darwin described as adaptations? I think God has never stopped creating;

the process continues. He put in us the ability to become better. I feel that God is too great to have an end to His imagination, His creativity. Psalm 104: 24 reads, "O Lord, how manifold are thy works! In wisdom hast thou made them all; the earth is full of thy riches." The world is full of diversity. Even though we call it diversity, it is simply His wise imagination. As the world turns and life continues, we will see more of it. Everything He created in his infinite wisdom had and has a purpose. He created them in wisdom. He knew and knows just what He is doing. For example, the foraminifera, microorganisms that existed in the Cambrian Period of the Paleozoic Era, now extinct, secreted ooze which is the oil we use as fuel today. Also consider the massive trees of Pennsylvanian and Mississippian Periods near the end of the Paleozoic Era, which formed the coal we mine today. The size of Earth is limited and changes in species are necessary to maintain the amount of matter on the planet. Psalm 104: 29,30 states, ".. thou takest away their breath; they die, and return to their dust. Thou sendest forth thy spirit, they are created: thou renewest the face of the earth."

In addition to His wisdom, how boring would this world be if there were no changes? If God had not interrupted creation with extinctions, what might the conditions be on Earth today?

My Thoughts:

Extinctions that have occurred has been for the good of man. Even the present changes are for our good. If there had not been extinctions our environment may not be in a suitable state.

Of all the things that have changed, are changing and will change, I am glad to know that God never changed, is not changing and will not change. In Malachi 3: 6, God says, "For I am the LORD, I change not; therefore ye sons of

Jacob are not consumed." This suggests that if God changes we would perish. Thank God for His immutability.

Your Thoughts:

_____

_____

_____

_____

_____

_____

_____

14. ANY ONE OF THOSE STONES WOULD WORK

"And he took his staff in his hand, and chose him five smooth stones out of the brook, and put them in a shepherd's bag which he had, even in a scrip; and his sling was in his hand: and he drew near to the Philistine."
I Samuel 17: 40

The story of David and Goliath is well-known. It is the story of a young boy, David, who accepted the challenge of a giant, Goliath. Well trained soldiers were afraid as the Goliath yelled daily, "Give me a man!"

David chose to go up against a giant with a sling and five smooth stones. David's only experiences included hand to hand battle with a bear and a lion. He accredited his victories to the God of Israel. His sling shot was probably used to scare off predators as he watched his father's sheep.

How could David be so confident? First, he was confident that the God of Israel was on his side. Second, Goliath was uncircumcised and was threatening the army of God. And third, he had chosen 5 smooth stones that had undergone the trials of nature.

The stones were taken from a brook. The smoothness came from weathering which included being beat against other rocks as it traveled down the brook. The stones had proven they would stay together when hitting a target and for this reason they were chosen. All the stones were smooth and any one of those stones would have worked.

71

While you may not have had to fight a physical giant, you most certainly have had to fight a spiritual one(s). What weapon(s) did you choose … prayer, fasting, praise, etc.? Did you find that any one of them would work?

My Thoughts:

We can see in scripture where spiritual weapons have been successful in fighting situations that seem as though change is nowhere in sight.

Leah used praise to bring forth Judah. Hannah used prayer to give birth to Samuel. Ester used fasting to save a nation. Woman with the issue of blood used her faith to be healed. There are so many stories that could be used as a reference to show that a change will come.

As it is in the natural so it is in the spirit. Since a rock is a conglomerate of materials, a combination of spiritual weapons could be used as well.

Your Thoughts:

_____

_____

_____

_____

_____

_____

15. ORDAINED WITH DESTINY

"Honor thy father and thy mother: that thy
days may be long upon the land in which
the LORD thy God giveth thee."
Exodus 20: 12

God commanded us to honor our parents. Life is shortened when this commandment is broken. To dishonor your parents is to question God. For it was God who chose your parents having the right set of genes for you to become the unique individual fulfilling your purpose.

In the book of Jeremiah, there was a need for a prophet to bring a word from God to the stubborn people of Judah. God chose Jeremiah. He chose when he would enter time, He gave him purpose, and the parents with the necessary DNA to produce this prophet. For He told Jeremiah (Jeremiah 1:5), "Before I formed thee in the belly I knew thee; and before thou camest forth out of the womb I sanctified thee and I ordained thee a prophet unto the nations."

Just like Jeremiah, we were known, given purpose, and given the right parents to fulfill our destiny. God was deliberate in bringing us into this world at this time.

God said in Jeremiah 29: 11, "For I know the thoughts that I think toward you, saith the Lord, thoughts of peace, and not of evil, to give you an expected end."

What are your gifts, your talents that you have that you think will help you fulfill your destiny?

My Thoughts:

I thank God for my parents, who taught me compassion throughout my life. Their DNA has given me an extraordinary love for people and a sincere desire for them to succeed. This love for people is expressed in my God given gift to teach. Writing this book comes out of that gift. My gift is genuine, but most importantly, my desire is for ALL to receive the gift of salvation.

Your Thoughts:

_____

_____

_____

_____

_____

_____

16. HIDDEN BEAUTY

*"And why take ye thought for raiment? Consider
the lilies of the field, how they grow; they toil not,
neither do they spin: And yet I say unto you, That even
Solomon in all his glory was not arrayed like one of
these, Wherefore, if God so clothe the grass of the field,
which today is and tomorrow is cast into the oven, shall
he not much more clothe you, O ye of little faith."*
Matthew 6: 28 – 30

In an advanced botany class, I observed the hair on the filament of a stamen within a flower. I noticed that each hair was one single cell that looked like a string of pearls. It was breathtaking! If need is what's driving evolution, what would be the purpose of this hidden beauty? Does the hair have to be beautiful to fulfill its purpose?

In I Kings, when the queen of Sheba had seen King Solomon's possessions, it rendered her breathless. God said that with all of Solomon's wisdom, the house that he built, the meat on his table, the sitting of his servants, the attendance of his ministers, their apparel, his cupbearers, and the ascent by which he went up unto the house of the LORD was not bedecked like the lilies of the field.

I believe there are more hidden beauties that our present generation will not see or discover but future generations will enjoy and have a greater understanding of our Divine Designer.

Modern technology has allowed us to see God in a new and more profound way. How could this technology and modern science be used to spread the gospel?

My Thoughts:

I feel that technology will advance to the point where it will give witness to God's existence. In the search for bigger, better, and faster God will be found! Today we spread the Gospel through television, Facebook, and other means. As scientists and technicians advance in their work and learn there has to be a mind greater than man, they will become the ones that will declare His existence. Atheists, evolutionists, naturalists, and agnostics will proclaim His existence.

Your Thoughts:

_____

_____

_____

_____

_____

_____

CONCLUSION: AN ENCOUNTER WITH THE TRUTH

Several renowned Christian personalities have stated that the most important question that could be asked is, "What is Truth?" It is what we wrap our reality around. If what we believe is not the truth then our reality is distorted. It influences how we see people and circumstances.

The truth for many has become a feeling rather than reality. We must remember that feelings change. If truth is based on feelings, what happens to truth when feelings change? Feelings will change just as sure as someone is engaged with people and in their environment.

The Russian physicist who created the Russian atomic bomb said the truth is more powerful than a bomb. I wonder how the physicist knowing the strength of an atomic bomb, came to such a profound conclusion. Could he have experienced a similar encounter with God like I had that night on my knees in the chapel on my college campus?

In the seventeenth chapter of I Samuel, David had several encounters that would so establish his knowledge of truth that he would fight a well-trained, fully dressed in armor, weapon carrying Giant with a sling shot and a stone.

David courageous acts were based on his knowledge of the truth, but Joseph, the son of Jacob and Rachel, paid attention to the strategy of God. Joseph's story begins in the thirty-seventh chapter of Genesis and completes the book. Many have preached his life, "From the Pit to the Palace". Joseph knew God had given him a dream and with all that he was going through, he was to fulfill the dream. He said to his brothers, "Now therefore be not grieved, nor angry with yourselves, that ye sold me hither: for God did send me before you to preserve life.….And God sent me before you to preserve you a posterity in the earth, and to save your lives by a great deliverance. So now it was not you that sent me hither, but God: …" Joseph saw this all as a strategic plan of God.

I employ you to seek the truth and have encounters for yourself. Pay attention to the strategies of the Creator not only in what you read, but in your life. Watch how something that occurred in your life which seemingly made no sense revealed itself as intentional and relevant. The word of God declares the truth will make you free because Jesus is the way, the TRUTH, and the life.

ART CREDITS

All drawings done by the author

ACKNOWLEGEMENTS

Thank you **Patricia Crump McRae** for your continued encouragement. You have been a constant source of strength. You have never withheld the truth and it is appreciated.

Thank you **Ernest Lavon Stephens I,** my husband. Your presence always means a lot.

Thank you **Sadarryle Evette Stephens**, my daughter. You have constantly pushed me. You have been with me through the thick and the thin. And I share this accomplishment with you.

Thank you **Ernest Lavon Stephens II**, my son. You stirred me in the right direction. I do not take for granted your insight and concern.

Thank you **Taurean Tamar Stephens**, my son. Your love speaks volumes. Your "always" at the end of our conversations gives me reassurance that it all is well.

Thank you **Bishop Michael Anthony Blue I**, my pastor. The example you set and the lessons you have taught have given me the determination to continue this path I believe God has ordained for me. May God continue to give you influence over many.

BIBLIOGRAPHY

King James Version. Zondervan: Grand Rapids, Mich., 1987.

1. IN THE BEGINNING

[1] *Origins of the Universe."* National Geographic Society, 1996-2010.

5. EARTH'S POSITION

[2] *"Reasons To Believe."* Dr. Hugh Ross et al. Trinity Broadcasting Network: Santa Ana, California. Broadcast February 20, 2010.

9. NO JUNK DNA

[3] *"Reasons To Believe."* Dr. Hugh Ross et al. Trinity Broadcasting Network: Santa Ana. California. Broadcast May 1, 2010.

10. LEFT HANDED AMINO ACIDS

[4] Biggs, Alton and et al. *Biology: The Dynamics of Life.* Glencoe/McGraw Hill: Columbus, Ohio, 2000, p. 390.

Printed in the United States
By Bookmasters